VELOCIRAPTOR

by Laura K. Murray

Consultant: Mathew J. Wedel, PhD
Western University of Health Sciences
Pomona, California

PEBBLE
a capstone imprint

Published by Pebble, an imprint of Capstone
1710 Roe Crest Drive, North Mankato, Minnesota 56003
capstonepub.com

Copyright © 2025 by Capstone. All rights reserved. No part of this publication may be reproduced in whole or in part, or stored in a retrieval system, or transmitted in any form or by any means, electronic, mechanical, photocopying, recording, or otherwise, without written permission of the publisher.

Library of Congress Cataloging-in-Publication Data
Names: Murray, Laura K., 1989– author.
Title: Velociraptor / by Laura K. Murray.
Description: North Mankato, Minnesota : Pebble, an imprint of Capstone, [2025] | Series: Dinosaur guides | Includes bibliographical references and index. | Audience: Ages 5–8 | Audience: Grades 2–3 | Summary: "Readers will love digging into this book all about Velociraptor! Engaging text and images make it a great choice for information to use in a report or just to read for fun"—Provided by publisher.
Identifiers: LCCN 2024021137 (print) | LCCN 2024021138 (ebook) | ISBN 9780756589158 (hardcover) | ISBN 9780756589424 (paperback) | ISBN 9780756589196 (pdf) | ISBN 9780756589448 (kindle edition) | ISBN 9780756589431 (epub)
Subjects: LCSH: Velociraptor—Juvenile literature.
Classification: LCC QE862.S3 M888 2025 (print) | LCC QE862.S3 (ebook) | DDC 567.912—dc23/eng/20240524
LC record available at https://lccn.loc.gov/2024021137
LC ebook record available at https://lccn.loc.gov/2024021138

Editorial Credits
Editor: Erika L. Shores; Designer: Dina Her; Media Researcher: Jo Miller; Production Specialist: Tori Abraham

Image Credits
Alamy: Collection Christophel, 25, PhotoStock-Israel, 9, Wolfgang Kaehler, 24, ZUMA Press, Inc., 28; Bridgeman Images: Patrice Cartier, 20; Capstone: Jon Hughes, cover, 6, 12, 15, 17, 19, 23; Getty Images: Daniel Eskridge/Stocktrek Images, 1, 11, Stocktrek Images, 5; Science Source: MARK P. WITTON, 18; Shutterstock: Kues, background (throughout), RobNaw, 8; Superstock: Francois Gohier/Mary Evans Picture Library, 27

Any additional websites and resources referenced in this book are not maintained, authorized, or sponsored by Capstone. All product and company names are trademarks™ or registered® trademarks of their respective holders.

Printed and bound in China.   6098

Table of Contents

Fast Raptor 4

Where in the World 7

Velociraptor Bodies 10

What Velociraptor Ate 16

Life of Velociraptor 21

Discovering Velociraptor 26

    Fast Facts 29

    Glossary 30

    Read More 31

    Internet Sites 31

    Index 32

    About the Author 32

Words in **bold** are in the glossary.

Fast Raptor

What small, fast dinosaur had feathers? Velociraptor! Its name means "**swift** thief." It was about the size of a turkey. It may have looked like an odd kind of bird. But it could not fly. It ran on two legs.

Velociraptor lived about 74 to 70 million years ago. That was during the Late Cretaceous Period. Velociraptors are often called raptors. There are other dinosaurs in the raptor group too.

Where in the World

Velociraptor lived in east and central Asia. Today, the area is the Gobi Desert. It stretches across southern Mongolia and northern China.

Velociraptor roamed the warm and dry area. The land was full of wildlife and plants. There were big sand dunes. There were low valleys. There weren't many trees. Water only flowed in a few rivers and streams.

The area where Velociraptor lived was home to many dinosaurs. Many dinosaur **fossils** are found there. Scientists go there to study the fossils of Velociraptors and other dinosaurs. Fossils help people learn about life millions of years ago.

Gobi Desert

fossils of Oviraptor eggs

In 1923, a paleontologist found the first dinosaur egg nests in the Gobi Desert. The eggs came from Oviraptor. The eggs showed that some dinosaurs acted like birds.

Velociraptor Bodies

Velociraptor weighed about 43 pounds (20 kilograms). It was about 6.5 feet (2 meters) long. Velociraptor had a long, narrow skull. Its strong jaw and sharp teeth ripped apart **prey**.

Velociraptor was fast! It could reach speeds of 25 miles (40 kilometers) per hour. Strong legs helped it run. A long, stiff tail helped it steer. Velociraptor used its tail to balance and turn quickly.

Velociraptor walked on two legs. It had large feet. Each foot had three toes. Velociraptor walked with two toes on the ground. Its other toe stuck up straight. It is called the toe claw or sickle claw.

Toe claws were deadly weapons. They could grow to 2.5 inches (6.4 centimeters). They were like hooks. Velociraptor likely used its toe claw to stab prey. It kept the prey from escaping.

Velociraptor had feathers. Its arms looked like wings. But it could not fly. Its arms were too short. It did not have big enough arm muscles to fly.

Feathers may have helped Velociraptor show off to **mates**. They may have helped it steer while running. They may have helped with warmth too. Scientists think baby Velociraptors may have been light enough to fly.

What Velociraptor Ate

Velociraptor was a meat eater. It likely ate smaller dinosaurs and **mammals**. It ate lizards and other reptiles. It may have hunted baby dinosaurs, such as Oviraptors or Protoceratops. It may have even eaten baby Velociraptors. Velociraptor could have eaten the eggs of other animals too.

Did You Know?

Velociraptor teeth curved backward. They held prey tight. When Velociraptor lost teeth, new, sharp teeth grew in.

Velociraptor likely had a very good sense of smell. This was helpful for hunting. Velociraptor chased down its prey. It used its hand claws and teeth to grab its meal. Then Velociraptor killed its prey with its large toe claw.

Velociraptor may have eaten the remains of larger animals. Fossils show that some Velociraptors ate bigger dinosaurs. Scientists think they ate dinosaurs that were already dead.

Life of Velociraptor

A Velociraptor was born from an egg. An adult Velociraptor took care of the eggs. It may have acted like a chicken. It tried to keep the nest and eggs safe.

Velociraptor may have used its feathers to keep the eggs warm. It likely covered its nest with its arms.

Velociraptor had to watch out for **predators**. Larger, meat-eating dinosaurs hunted Velociraptor. Giant flying reptiles could have hunted it from the air.

Scientists do not know if Velociraptors lived alone or in groups. It is likely they acted alone. They may have hunted or traveled together. But scientists have not found **proof** of this.

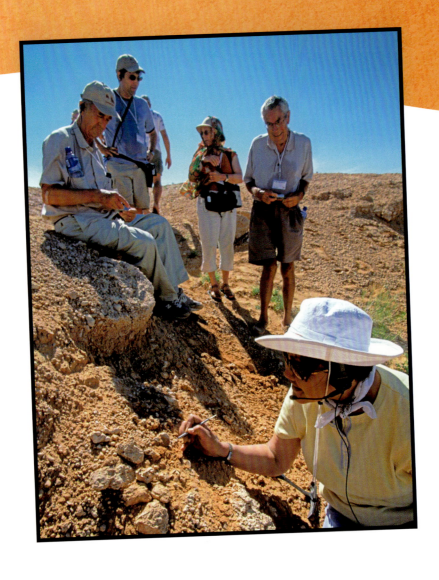

Today, scientists put Velociraptor in two groups. The first group has been found in Mongolia. The second group has been found in China.

Velociraptor has been shown in famous movies. But the movies do not get everything correct. Velociraptors in movies are often much bigger than they were in real life. They usually do not have feathers.

Did You Know?
Velociraptors in the Jurassic World movies were based on the much larger Deinonychus.

Discovering Velociraptor

The first Velociraptor fossil was found in 1923. It was a crushed skull. Peter Kaisen found the fossil in the Gobi Desert. In 1924, Henry Fairfield Osborn named Velociraptor.

In 1971, paleontologists found one of the most famous dinosaur fossils ever. It is a Velociraptor fighting with a Protoceratops. The Velociraptor is stabbing its claw into the other dinosaur. The Protoceratops is biting the Velociraptor's arm.

Did You Know?

Scientists think the fighting dinosaurs were buried alive. They may have died during a sandstorm or from a sand dune falling on them.

In 2007, scientists shared important news. They had studied a Velociraptor fossil discovered in Mongolia in 1998. This bone had little bumps on it. The bumps were the places that feathers grew. Many birds have the same kind of bones. The fossil proved that Velociraptor had feathers.

Today, people still study the Velociraptor. They ask questions. They look for clues about how Velociraptor lived. There is a lot left to learn about these amazing, feathered dinosaurs!

Fast Facts

Name: Velociraptor (meaning "swift thief")

Lived: Late Cretaceous Period (about 74 to 70 million years ago)

Range: central and eastern Asia in China and Mongolia

Habitat: warm, dry areas with big sand dunes and low valleys

Food: small mammals, reptiles, baby dinosaurs, dinosaur eggs, remains of dead animals

Threats: large, meat-eating dinosaurs, giant flying reptiles

Discovered: 1923, Gobi Desert

Glossary

fossil (FAH-suhl)—the remains or traces of a living thing from many years ago

mammal (MAM-uhl)—a warm-blooded animal that has hair or fur; they usually give birth to live young

mate (MAYT)—a partner that joins with another to produce young

predator (PRED-uh-tur)—an animal that hunts other animals for food

prey (PRAY)—an animal that is hunted or killed by another animal for food

proof (PROOF)—something that helps show the truth or fact

swift (SWIFT)—fast

Read More

Finn, Peter. *The Fierce Velociraptor*. New York: Enslow Publishing, 2022.

Lomax, Dean R. *My Book of Fossils*. New York: DK Publishing, 2022.

Vonder Brink, Tracy. *The Velociraptor*. New York: Crabtree Publishing, 2024.

Internet Sites

American Museum of Natural History: Dinosaur Facts
amnh.org/dinosaurs/dinosaur-facts

National Geographic Kids: Velociraptor
kids.nationalgeographic.com/animals/prehistoric/facts/velociraptor

Natural History Museum: Velociraptor
nhm.ac.uk/discover/dino-directory/velociraptor.html

Index

discovery, 26, 29

eggs, 9, 16, 21

feathers, 4, 14, 21, 25, 28
fossils, 8, 19, 26, 28

legs, 4, 10, 13

mates, 14

name, 4, 26, 29

predators, 22, 29
prey, 10, 13, 16, 17, 18, 29

size, 4, 10, 25

tails, 10
teeth, 10, 17, 18
toe claws, 13, 18, 26

when it lived, 4, 29
where it lived, 7, 8, 29

About the Author

Laura K. Murray is the Minnesota-based author of more than 100 books for young readers. She loves learning from fellow readers and helping others find their reading superpowers! Visit LauraKMurray.com.